Title: "Social Media Marketing Future: Navigating the Next Decade"

This book, along with its contents encompassing text, illustrations, images, diagrams, and other creative elements, is the exclusive property of FAISAL JAMIL and is safeguarded by copyright law.

FAISAL JAMIL asserts full ownership and retains all rights to this book. No part of this publication may be reproduced, distributed, or transmitted in any form or by any means, such as photocopying, recording, or electronic methods, without prior written consent from the copyright holder. Brief quotations in critical reviews and certain noncommercial uses permitted by copyright law are exceptions.

This copyright notice applies to all editions, formats, and translations of the book, whether in print, digital, or any other medium or technology existing now or developed in the future. Unauthorized use or infringement may result in legal action and pursuit of remedies under applicable copyright laws.

While efforts have been made to ensure accuracy and reliability, FAISAL JAMIL does not guarantee the completeness or suitability of the information. Readers are responsible for evaluating and using the content judiciously.

FAISAL JAMIL reserves the right to make changes, updates, or corrections to the book without prior notice. Inclusion of

Warm regards,

FAISAL JAMIL

I Always Give's Free Copies Need Your Feedback And

Reviews Keeps In Touch!

http://www.amazon.com/author/faisal.jamil

Email: faisaljamilauthor@gmail.com

About the author

Certainly! Faisal Jamil is a multifaceted individual with a diverse set of skills and experiences. With a strong foundation in computer knowledge since childhood, he has developed a deep understanding of technology that informs his work as a content writer. Faisal also possesses digital skills, which further enhance his abilities in various digital platforms and technologies.

Beyond his professional endeavors, Faisal Jamil has also excelled in the martial arts, particularly Shotokan Karate, where he achieved the prestigious rank of first Dan black belt. This achievement speaks to his dedication, discipline, and commitment to personal growth and mastery.

In his professional life, Faisal Jamil has carved out a successful career in sales management within the Fast Moving Consumer Goods (FMCG) sector. His roles in various FMCG companies have honed his skills in strategic planning, team leadership, and business development. Faisal's ability to drive sales and achieve targets has been instrumental in his career progression, showcasing his talent for identifying opportunities and delivering results.

Faisal Jamil is also deeply interested in business investment strategies, planning, and execution. His understanding of these areas has been key to his success in the business world, allowing him to make informed decisions and implement effective strategies. His ability to navigate the complexities of investment planning and execution has set him apart as a strategic thinker and a valuable asset in any business endeavor.

Overall, Faisal Jamil is a dynamic individual who combines his passion for technology, martial arts, sales management, digital skills, and business investment strategies to achieve success in diverse fields. His journey is a testament to his versatility, resilience, and continuous pursuit of excellence.

Yours Sincerely

FAISAL JAMIL

I Always Give's Free Copies Need Your Feedback And

Reviews Keeps In Touch!

https://www.amazon.com/author/faisal.jamil

Email: faisaljamilauthor@gmail.com

SOCIAL MEDIA MARKETING

FUTURE

NAVIGATING THE NEXT DECADE

Table of Content

INTRODUCTION

In an era where digital connectivity shapes every facet of our lives, social media has become the heartbeat of modern communication. As platforms evolve at lightning speed, marketers are constantly challenged to stay ahead of the curve, adapting to new technologies and trends that redefine how brands engage with their audiences. "Social Media Marketing Future: Navigating the Next Decade" is a comprehensive guide designed to equip marketers, business leaders, and social media enthusiasts with the insights and tools needed to thrive in this dynamic landscape.

The journey of social media marketing is one of rapid evolution. What began as simple text-based interactions on forums and blogs has transformed into a rich, multimedia-driven experience, epitomized by platforms like Instagram, TikTok, and YouTube. This book delves into the historical progression of social media, highlighting the pivotal technological advancements that have driven this change. From the rise of high-speed internet and mobile devices to the integration of artificial intelligence (AI), these innovations have not only expanded the capabilities of social media platforms but also reshaped user engagement and behavior.

As we navigate through the next decade, emerging technologies such as AI, augmented reality (AR), virtual reality (VR), and blockchain are poised to revolutionize the way we approach social media marketing. This book explores how these technologies are currently being utilized and their potential future applications. AI-driven chatbots, personalized content recommendations, immersive brand experiences through AR and VR, and enhanced data security with blockchain are just a few of the innovations that will redefine marketing strategies.

Consumer behavior is also undergoing significant shifts. Privacy concerns and demands for transparency are becoming more prominent, influencing how brands interact with their audiences. The rise of social commerce is transforming platforms into seamless shopping experiences, while user-generated content (UGC) continues to play a crucial role in building brand authenticity and engagement. This book provides a deep dive into these trends, offering strategies to leverage them effectively.

The landscape of social media platforms is becoming increasingly diverse. New and niche platforms are emerging, catering to specific interests and communities. Video content is dominating the digital space, with both short-form and long-form videos proving to be powerful tools for engagement. Understanding the impact of algorithm changes and adapting strategies accordingly is essential for maintaining visibility and driving success in this competitive environment.

Ethical considerations and social responsibility are more critical than ever. The spread of misinformation, the need for diversity and inclusion, and the balance between profit and purpose are issues that marketers must address head-on. This book provides strategies for tackling these challenges, promoting ethical practices, and aligning marketing efforts with broader social and environmental goals.

"Social Media Marketing Future: Navigating the Next Decade" is not just a guide to understanding the current state of social media marketing; it is a forward-looking exploration of what lies ahead. By staying informed and adaptable, marketers can create impactful, sustainable strategies that resonate with their audiences and drive long-term success in the ever-changing digital landscape. Join us on this journey to navigate the future of social media marketing and unlock the potential of the next decade.

Chapter 1

The Evolution of
Social Media Marketing

Branch 1: From Text to Multimedia

Historical Perspective

The journey of social media marketing began with text-based platforms, such as early internet forums and blogs, where individuals shared thoughts and information in a textual format. Platforms like MySpace and LiveJournal were among the first to capitalize on this, allowing users to create personal profiles and blogs, fostering communities around shared interests.

As the internet evolved, so did the complexity and capabilities of social media platforms. The introduction of multimedia elements marked a significant shift. Photo-sharing became prominent with the rise of Flickr and later Instagram, which launched in 2010, offering an easy way to share high-quality images with friends and followers. The evolution continued with platforms like YouTube (2005) and Vine (2013), which emphasized video content, leading to the current dominance of video-centric platforms like TikTok (2016).

The transition from text to multimedia significantly transformed social media marketing, making it more visually engaging and dynamic. This evolution enabled brands to tell their stories more compellingly, using a combination of images, videos, and interactive content to capture audience attention.

Technological Advancements

Several technological advancements have driven the evolution from text to multimedia in social media marketing:

Faster Internet Speeds: The development of broadband and fiber-optic internet connections allowed for quicker uploading and downloading of large multimedia files. This enabled the seamless streaming of high-definition videos and the sharing of high-resolution images.

Mobile Device Proliferation: The widespread adoption of smartphones and tablets equipped with advanced cameras and high-speed internet connectivity revolutionized social media usage. Mobile apps made it easier to create, upload, and consume multimedia content on the go.

Rise of AI: Artificial Intelligence (AI) has played a pivotal role in enhancing user experience on social media platforms. AI algorithms curate personalized content feeds, optimize ad targeting, and enable features like facial recognition in photos and videos. Additionally, AI-driven tools facilitate content creation, such as automated video editing and photo enhancements.

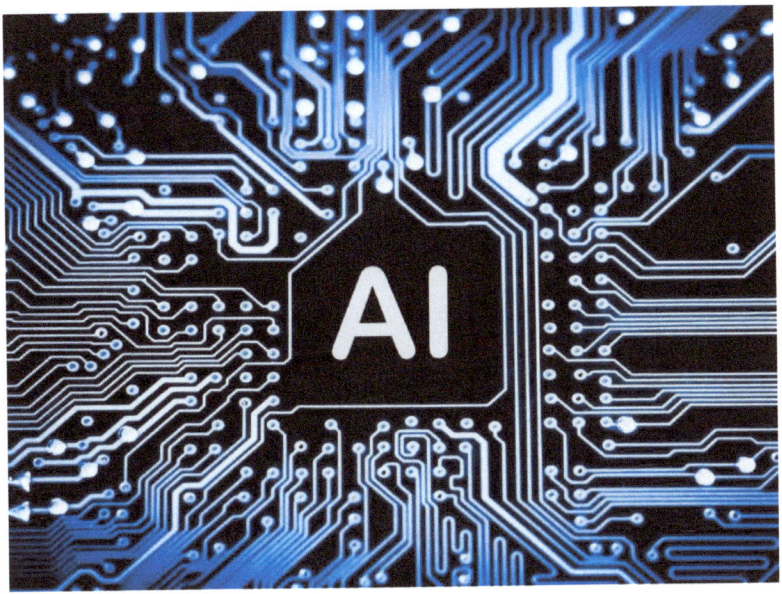

User Engagement

The shift from text to multimedia has profoundly impacted user engagement and behavior:

Increased Interaction: Multimedia content, being more visually appealing, encourages higher levels of interaction. Users are more likely to like, comment on, and share photos and videos compared to text-based posts.

Emotional Connection: Visual content, especially videos, can evoke stronger emotional responses. This emotional connection fosters deeper engagement and brand loyalty.

Immersive Experiences: Features like live streaming, 360-degree videos, and augmented reality (AR) filters provide immersive experiences that text alone cannot offer. These features enhance user engagement by making social media interactions more dynamic and interactive.

Content Consumption Patterns: The rise of short-form video content on platforms like TikTok has shifted how users consume content. Bite-sized, entertaining videos cater to shorter attention spans and are more likely to be consumed in large quantities.

Branch 2: The Rise of Influencer Marketing

Early Days

Influencer marketing has its roots in the early days of blogging and YouTube, where individuals with niche followings began to attract attention from brands. Initially, these influencers were often hobbyists or enthusiasts who shared their expertise and passions with a dedicated audience.

Grassroots Endorsements: Early influencer marketing was characterized by grassroots endorsements, where influencers promoted products they genuinely liked without any formal agreements or compensation. This authenticity resonated with audiences and established trust.

Blogger Collaborations: Brands began to recognize the potential of influencers to reach specific demographics. Collaborations with bloggers and YouTubers became more common, with brands sending free products for review or sponsoring content.

Current Landscape

Today, influencer marketing is a multi-billion dollar industry, integral to many brands' marketing strategies:

Key Players: Influencers now range from celebrities and mega-influencers with millions of followers to micro-influencers with smaller but highly engaged audiences. Platforms like Instagram, YouTube, and TikTok are hotspots for influencer activity.

Platforms and Strategies: Brands use a variety of strategies to leverage influencers, including sponsored posts, product placements, brand ambassadorships, and affiliate marketing. Platforms have also introduced features to facilitate influencer collaborations, such as Instagram's branded content tools.

Measurement and ROI:

The effectiveness of influencer campaigns is measured using various metrics, such as engagement rates, reach, and return on investment (ROI). Tools like social media analytics platforms and influencer marketing software help brands track and optimize their campaigns.

Future Trends

Several trends are likely to shape the future of influencer marketing:

Micro-Influencers: There is a growing shift towards collaborating with micro-influencers, who, despite having smaller followings, often boast higher engagement rates and more niche audiences. This trend is driven by the desire for authenticity and more targeted marketing.

Authenticity: Consumers are becoming more discerning, valuing authentic endorsements over obvious paid promotions. Influencers who maintain transparency and genuine connections with their audience will continue to thrive.

Emerging Platforms: As new social media platforms emerge, influencers will diversify their presence. Platforms like Clubhouse and emerging short-form video apps are gaining traction and could become new hubs for influencer marketing.

Branch 3: The Impact of Data Analytics

Introduction to Social Media Analytics

Social media analytics involves collecting and analyzing data from social media platforms to inform marketing strategies and business decisions. It encompasses various metrics, such as engagement rates, follower growth, and sentiment analysis.

Importance in Modern Marketing: Social media analytics is crucial for understanding audience behavior, measuring campaign effectiveness, and optimizing content strategies. It allows brands to make data-driven decisions, ensuring that their marketing efforts are aligned with their goals and resonate with their target audience.

Tools and Techniques

Several tools and techniques are used to gather and analyze social media data:

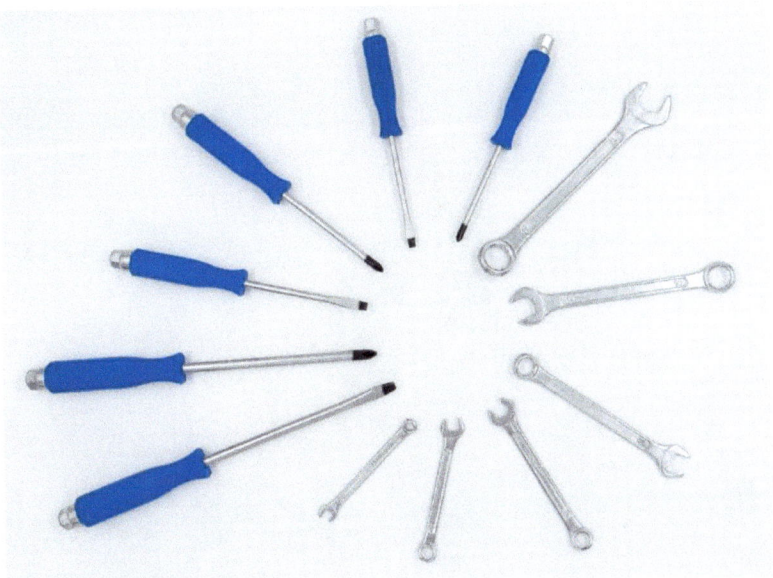

Sentiment Analysis: This technique involves analyzing text to determine the sentiment behind social media mentions, whether positive, negative, or neutral. Tools like Hootsuite Insights and Brandwatch provide sentiment analysis capabilities.

Predictive Analytics: Predictive analytics uses historical data to forecast future trends and behaviors. In social media marketing, it can predict which types of content are likely to perform well or which audience segments are most likely to engage with a campaign.

Engagement Metrics: Tools like Sprout Social, Buffer, and Google Analytics track various engagement metrics, including likes, shares, comments, and click-through rates. These metrics help brands understand what content resonates with their audience and refine their strategies accordingly.

Future Innovations

The future of social media analytics is poised for exciting innovations:

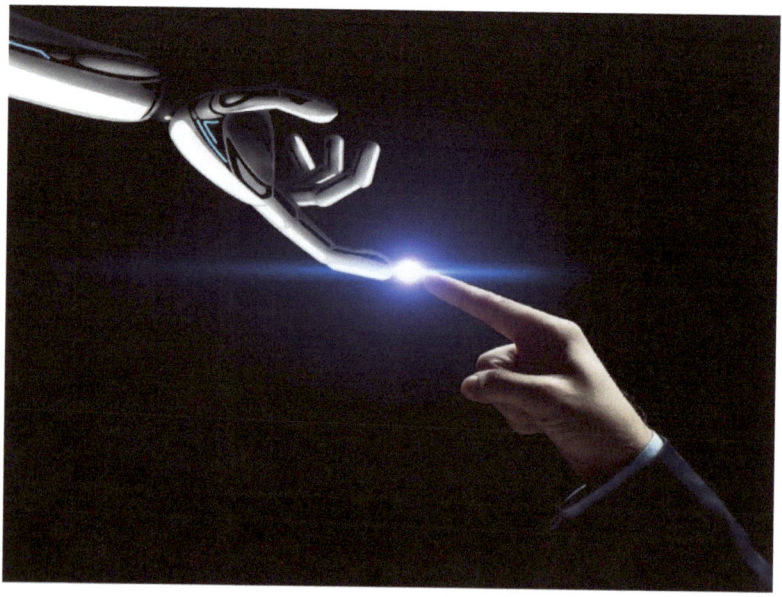

Real-Time Data Integration: Future analytics platforms will offer more advanced real-time data integration, allowing brands to monitor and respond to social media activity instantly. This will enable more agile and responsive marketing strategies.

AI-Driven Insights: Artificial intelligence will play a bigger role in social media analytics, providing deeper insights and automating complex analyses. AI can identify patterns and trends that might be missed by human analysts, offering more accurate and actionable recommendations.

Holistic View of Customer Journey: Future analytics tools will provide a more holistic view of the customer journey, integrating data from various touchpoints beyond social media. This comprehensive perspective will help brands understand the full impact of their social media efforts on overall business performance.

Chapter 2

Emerging Technologies in Social Media Marketing

Branch 1: Artificial Intelligence and Machine Learning

Current Applications

Artificial Intelligence (AI) and Machine Learning (ML) are revolutionizing social media marketing by automating processes, enhancing user experiences, and providing deeper insights:

Chatbots: AI-powered chatbots are used for customer service, automating responses to common queries, and providing personalized assistance. They are integrated into platforms like Facebook Messenger and WhatsApp, offering 24/7 support and improving customer satisfaction.

Personalized Content Recommendations: AI algorithms analyze user behavior and preferences to provide personalized content recommendations. Platforms like Instagram, YouTube, and TikTok use these algorithms to suggest posts, videos, and accounts that align with users' interests, increasing engagement and time spent on the platform.

Sentiment Analysis: AI-driven sentiment analysis tools monitor social media conversations to gauge public sentiment about brands, products, and services. This helps marketers understand audience perceptions and tailor their strategies accordingly.

Ad Targeting: Machine learning models optimize ad targeting by analyzing vast amounts of user data to predict which ads are most likely to resonate with specific audiences. This results in more effective campaigns and higher return on investment (ROI).

Content Creation: AI tools assist in content creation, from generating captions and hashtags to creating entire posts and articles. Tools like Copy.ai and Jasper.ai help marketers produce engaging content quickly.

Case Studies

Sephora: The beauty retailer uses AI-powered chatbots on Facebook Messenger to provide personalized beauty advice and product recommendations. This has enhanced customer engagement and increased sales by making the shopping experience more interactive and tailored to individual preferences.

Netflix: Known for its sophisticated recommendation system, Netflix uses machine learning to analyze viewing habits and recommend shows and movies. This personalized approach keeps users engaged and reduces churn.

Coca-Cola: Coca-Cola employs AI-driven sentiment analysis to monitor social media conversations about their products. This real-time feedback allows them to respond promptly to customer concerns and capitalize on positive trends.

Future Prospects

AI and machine learning will continue to transform social media marketing in several ways:

Advanced Natural Language Processing (NLP): Future advancements in NLP will enable more sophisticated chatbots and virtual assistants capable of understanding and responding to complex queries with greater accuracy and empathy.

Predictive Analytics: AI will enhance predictive analytics, allowing marketers to anticipate trends and consumer behavior more accurately. This will enable proactive marketing strategies and better allocation of resources.

Automated Video Creation: AI-powered tools will streamline video creation, making it easier for marketers to produce high-quality videos without extensive technical skills. This will include automated editing, script generation, and even synthetic actors.

Enhanced Personalization: AI will offer even more personalized user experiences, with hyper-targeted content and ads tailored to individual preferences and behaviors, leading to higher engagement and conversion rates.

Branch 2: Augmented Reality (AR) and Virtual Reality (VR)

Introduction to AR and VR

Augmented Reality (AR) and Virtual Reality (VR) are immersive technologies transforming how users interact with digital content:

Augmented Reality (AR): AR overlays digital information onto the real world, enhancing the user's environment with interactive elements. It is commonly experienced through smartphones, tablets, and AR glasses.

Virtual Reality (VR): VR creates a fully immersive digital environment that users can explore and interact with, typically using VR headsets and motion controllers. It provides a completely simulated experience, often used for gaming, training, and immersive storytelling.

Current Use Cases

AR and VR are already being utilized in various social media marketing applications:

Virtual Try-Ons: Brands like IKEA and L'Oréal use AR to allow users to virtually try on furniture or makeup products through their mobile apps or social media platforms. This enhances the shopping experience and reduces the likelihood of returns.

Immersive Brand Experiences: Companies like Coca-Cola and Nike create VR experiences that transport users to virtual worlds, offering immersive brand storytelling and interactive experiences that engage users on a deeper level.

Interactive Advertisements: AR-powered ads enable users to interact with products directly from their social media feeds. Snapchat and Instagram have AR filters that brands use to create engaging and interactive ad campaigns.

Future Potential

The future of AR and VR in social media marketing holds immense possibilities:

Fully Immersive Social Media Platforms: Social media platforms could evolve into fully immersive VR environments where users interact in virtual spaces. This would offer new opportunities for brands to create virtual storefronts, host events, and engage with audiences in innovative ways.

Integration of AR/VR in Everyday Interactions: As AR glasses and VR headsets become more mainstream, AR and

VR could be integrated into everyday social media interactions. This could include virtual meetups, AR-enhanced messaging, and mixed-reality content sharing.

Enhanced Data Visualization: AR and VR can be used to visualize data and analytics in more interactive and comprehensible ways. Marketers could use these tools to present campaign performance and insights in immersive formats, aiding in decision-making.

Branch 3: Blockchain and Decentralization

Understanding Blockchain

Blockchain is a decentralized digital ledger technology that records transactions across multiple computers in a secure and transparent manner:

Principles: Blockchain operates on principles of decentralization, transparency, and immutability. Each transaction is recorded in a block, and these blocks are linked together in a chain, making it difficult to alter or tamper with the data.

Smart Contracts: These are self-executing contracts with the terms directly written into code. They automatically enforce agreements and execute transactions when predetermined conditions are met.

Applications in Social Media

Blockchain has several potential applications in social media marketing:

Data Security: Blockchain can enhance data security by decentralizing data storage and ensuring that user data is protected from hacks and breaches. This can build trust with users who are increasingly concerned about data privacy.

Transparency: Blockchain can provide transparency in advertising by verifying the authenticity of ad metrics and ensuring that marketers are charged fairly for actual views and engagements. This can help combat ad fraud.

Decentralized Social Networks: Blockchain can enable the creation of decentralized social networks where users have greater control over their data and content. Platforms like Steemit and Minds are early examples of blockchain-based social networks.

Looking Ahead

The future of blockchain in social media marketing is promising:

Enhanced Trust and Accountability: Blockchain can enhance trust and accountability in social media interactions by providing verifiable records of transactions and engagements. This can be particularly useful for influencer marketing and ad verification.

Tokenization and Rewards: Blockchain can facilitate tokenization, allowing users to earn cryptocurrency or tokens for their contributions and engagement on social media platforms. This can incentivize content creation and active participation.

Interoperability and Data Portability: Blockchain can enable interoperability between different social media platforms, allowing users to seamlessly transfer their data and digital assets across multiple networks. This can create a more integrated and user-centric social media ecosystem.

Chapter 3

Consumer Behavior and Social Media Trends

Branch 1: The Shift Towards Privacy and Transparency

Privacy Concerns

As social media platforms have grown, so have concerns about privacy. High-profile data breaches and scandals, such as the Cambridge Analytica incident involving Facebook, have heightened awareness about how personal data is collected, stored, and used. These concerns have led to several notable changes in consumer behavior:

Increased Caution: Users are more cautious about sharing personal information online. They are more likely to adjust their privacy settings, limit the amount of data they share, and scrutinize the permissions they grant to apps and platforms.

Preference for Secure Platforms:

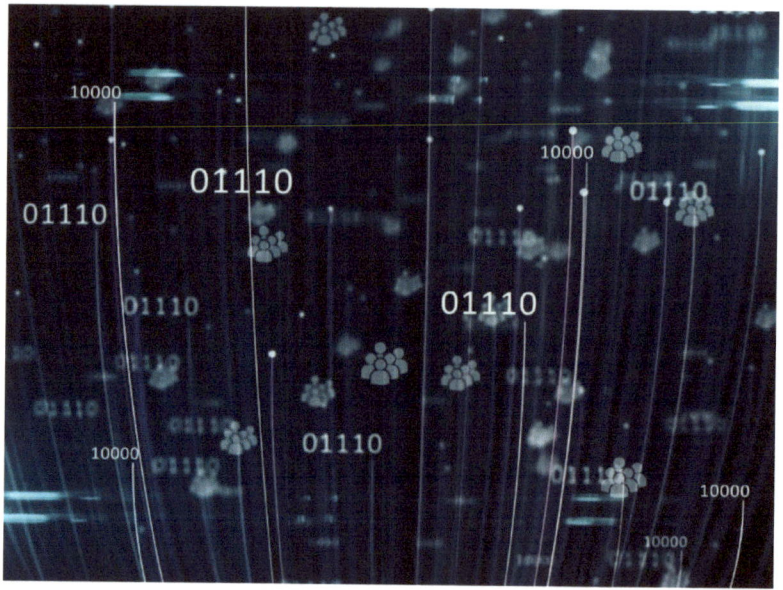

Consumers are gravitating towards platforms that prioritize data security and offer clear privacy policies. For instance, messaging apps like Signal and Telegram, which emphasize end-to-end encryption, have seen a rise in popularity.

Demand for Control: Users want more control over their data, including the ability to download, delete, and manage their information. This has led to the implementation of features like data portability and enhanced privacy settings across various platforms.

Transparency Demands

In addition to privacy, there is an increasing demand for transparency from both brands and social media companies. Consumers expect clear, honest communication about how their data is used and how companies operate:

Brand Authenticity: Consumers are drawn to brands that are transparent about their practices, values, and sourcing. They want to know where products come from, how they are made, and the impact on the environment and society.

Influencer Transparency: There is a growing expectation for influencers to disclose paid partnerships and sponsorships. Regulations, such as the Federal Trade

Commission (FTC) guidelines in the US, require influencers to clearly label sponsored content.

Platform Accountability: Social media platforms are under pressure to be transparent about their algorithms, content moderation policies, and data practices. Users want to understand how content is prioritized and why certain posts are flagged or removed.

Future Implications

These trends will significantly shape future marketing strategies:

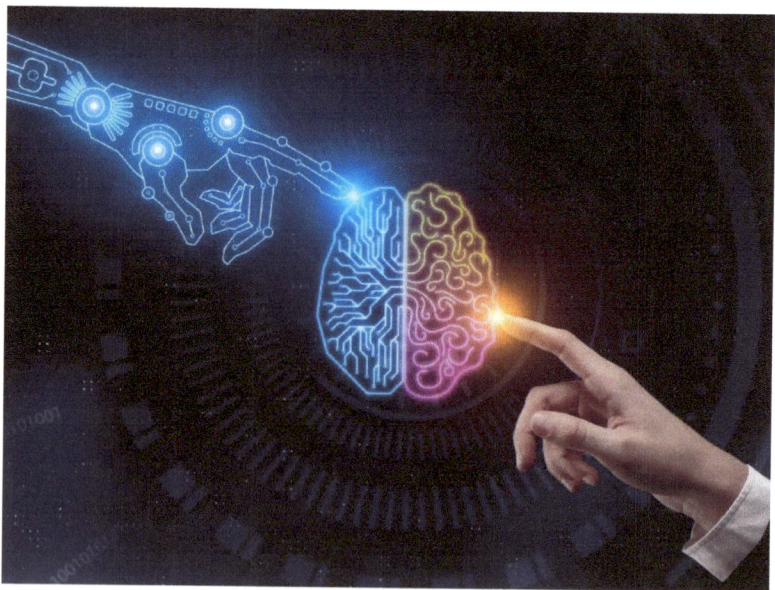

Ethical Data Practices: Brands will need to adopt ethical data practices, ensuring that they collect and use data responsibly and transparently. This includes obtaining explicit consent from users and being transparent about how data is used.

Transparent Communication: Clear and honest communication will become a cornerstone of brand strategy. Brands that build trust through transparency will foster stronger relationships with their audience.

Regulatory Compliance: Compliance with privacy regulations, such as the General Data Protection Regulation (GDPR) in Europe and the California Consumer Privacy Act (CCPA), will be crucial. Brands will need to stay updated on evolving regulations and ensure that their practices meet legal requirements.

Branch 2: The Growth of Social Commerce

Definition and Evolution

Social commerce refers to the use of social media platforms to facilitate online shopping and transactions. It has evolved from simple product recommendations and reviews shared by users to fully integrated e-commerce experiences within social media platforms:

Early Days: Initially, social commerce involved users sharing product reviews, recommendations, and links to online stores. This word-of-mouth marketing was powerful but limited in its scope and functionality.

Rise of Shoppable Posts: Platforms like Instagram and Pinterest introduced shoppable posts, allowing users to purchase products directly from posts without leaving the platform. This seamless integration simplified the buying process and boosted sales.

In-App Purchases: Social media platforms have incorporated in-app purchase features, enabling users to complete transactions within the app. Facebook Marketplace and Instagram Checkout are prime examples of this trend.

Platform Integration

Major social media platforms are continuously enhancing their e-commerce capabilities:

Instagram: Instagram Shopping allows brands to create shoppable posts and stories, while Instagram Checkout enables users to complete purchases within the app. The platform also features shopping tabs on profiles and the Explore page.

Facebook: Facebook Shops provide a customizable storefront for businesses, allowing users to browse and purchase products directly on the platform. Facebook Marketplace facilitates peer-to-peer buying and selling.

TikTok: TikTok has partnered with e-commerce platforms like Shopify to enable in-app shopping. The platform also features shoppable livestreams and product links in videos.

Pinterest: Pinterest's Shopping Ads and Catalogs allow brands to upload product catalogs and create shoppable pins. The platform's visual search technology also enhances the shopping experience.

Future Trends

Social commerce is poised for significant growth and innovation:

Live Shopping: Live shopping events, where influencers and brands showcase products in real-time and interact with viewers, are gaining popularity. This trend blends entertainment with e-commerce, creating an engaging shopping experience.

Personalized Shopping Experiences: Advances in AI and data analytics will enable more personalized shopping experiences. Social media platforms will use user data to recommend products tailored to individual preferences and behaviors.

Social Payment Solutions: Integrated payment solutions, such as Facebook Pay and WhatsApp Pay, will streamline transactions and enhance the social commerce experience. These solutions will facilitate quick and secure payments within social media apps.

Branch 3: The Role of User-Generated Content (UGC)

Importance of UGC

User-generated content (UGC) is any form of content created by users rather than brands. UGC is a powerful tool in social media marketing for several reasons:

Authenticity: UGC is perceived as more authentic and trustworthy than brand-generated content. When users share their experiences and reviews, it builds credibility and trust among other consumers.

Engagement: UGC drives higher engagement levels. Users are more likely to interact with content created by their peers, leading to increased likes, comments, shares, and overall visibility.

Community Building: Encouraging UGC fosters a sense of community and belonging. Brands that leverage UGC effectively can create a loyal and engaged customer base.

Strategies for Encouraging UGC

Brands can encourage and leverage UGC through various strategies:

Contests and Challenges: Running contests and challenges that invite users to create and share content related to the brand can generate a significant amount of UGC. For example, hashtag challenges on TikTok and Instagram encourage users to participate and share their entries.

Incentives and Rewards: Offering incentives, such as discounts, freebies, or features on the brand's social media pages, can motivate users to create and share content. Highlighting user content on official brand accounts also fosters engagement.

Community Building: Creating and nurturing online communities where users feel valued and heard can encourage UGC. Brands can use platforms like Facebook Groups, Reddit, or dedicated forums to build these communities.

Looking Forward

The future of UGC will be shaped by technological advancements and evolving consumer behavior:

AI in Content Creation and Curation: AI tools will assist in the creation and curation of UGC. For example, AI can generate content ideas, enhance user-generated photos and videos, and curate the most relevant and engaging UGC for brand use.

Enhanced Interactivity: Future UGC will likely become more interactive, incorporating elements like AR filters, VR experiences, and interactive storytelling. This will create more immersive and engaging content for users.

Integration with Social Commerce: UGC will play a crucial role in social commerce. Reviews, testimonials, and real-life product showcases by users will influence purchase decisions and enhance the overall shopping experience on social media platforms.

Chapter 4

The Changing Landscape of Social Media Platforms

Branch 1: Platform Diversification

New Entrants

The social media landscape is constantly evolving, with new platforms emerging to challenge established giants. These new entrants often bring innovative features and cater to specific user needs, which can significantly impact the marketing landscape:

Clubhouse: The audio-based social networking app gained popularity by offering live, voice-only conversations in various "rooms." Its rise highlighted the demand for more intimate and real-time interactions.

BeReal: This app encourages users to post one unfiltered photo per day, taken simultaneously, promoting authenticity and countering the curated nature of other platforms.

Vero: Positioned as a more user-centric social network, Vero emphasizes privacy and ad-free experiences, attracting users tired of traditional platforms' commercial focus.

Niche Platforms

Niche platforms catering to specific interests and communities are gaining traction, providing unique opportunities for marketers to target highly engaged audiences:

Goodreads: A social network for book lovers, where users can share reviews, recommendations, and join book clubs. It offers a targeted audience for authors and publishers.

Strava: A platform for athletes, particularly runners and cyclists, where users can track their activities, share their progress, and join challenges. Brands in the fitness and sports industry can leverage this platform for targeted campaigns.

Dribbble and Behance: These platforms cater to designers and creatives, allowing them to showcase their work and connect with potential clients. They offer a focused audience for brands in the creative industry.

Future Outlook

Platform diversification will continue to shape the social media landscape, leading to several implications for marketers:

Multi-Platform Strategies: Marketers will need to adopt multi-platform strategies to reach diverse audiences. This involves understanding the unique features and user demographics of each platform and tailoring content accordingly.

Specialized Content: Creating specialized content for niche platforms will become essential. Brands will need to engage deeply with specific communities and create content that resonates with their interests and values.

Agility and Adaptability: Staying agile and adaptable will be crucial as new platforms emerge and user preferences shift. Marketers will need to be quick to experiment with new platforms and integrate them into their broader strategies.

Branch 2: The Role of Video Content

Video Dominance

Video content has become the dominant form of content on social media platforms, driven by its engaging and visually appealing nature:

TikTok: Known for its short-form videos, TikTok has revolutionized content consumption with its algorithmically driven feed, prioritizing highly engaging and entertaining content.

YouTube: As the leading platform for long-form video content, YouTube remains a key player in video marketing, offering opportunities for in-depth tutorials, product reviews, and vlogs.

Instagram and Facebook: Both platforms have heavily integrated video content through features like Stories, IGTV, Reels, and Facebook Watch, catering to different content lengths and styles.

Short-Form vs. Long-Form

Comparing the popularity and effectiveness of short-form and long-form video content reveals insights into their respective roles in marketing strategies:

Short-Form Videos: Platforms like TikTok and Instagram Reels thrive on short-form content, typically ranging from 15 seconds to 1 minute. These videos are highly shareable, quick to consume, and perfect for capturing attention in a fast-paced digital environment.

Long-Form Videos: YouTube excels with long-form content, allowing for more comprehensive and in-depth storytelling.

This format is ideal for tutorials, detailed product reviews, and educational content, where longer engagement times are beneficial.

Future of Video Marketing

The future of video marketing will be shaped by several advancements and trends:

Video Production Technology: Innovations in video production technology, including AI-driven editing tools and high-quality mobile cameras, will make creating professional-grade videos more accessible to brands of all sizes.

Interactive Elements: The integration of interactive elements, such as clickable links, polls, and augmented reality (AR) features, will enhance viewer engagement and provide more immersive experiences.

Live Streaming: Live streaming will continue to grow, offering real-time interaction and engagement opportunities. Platforms like Twitch, YouTube Live, and Instagram Live will play significant roles in this trend.

Branch 3: The Impact of Algorithm Changes

Understanding Algorithms

Social media algorithms determine how content is displayed and prioritized in users' feeds. Understanding these algorithms is crucial for marketers aiming to maximize visibility and engagement:

Engagement-Based Algorithms: Most platforms prioritize content with higher engagement rates (likes, comments, shares). This means that posts that quickly generate interactions are more likely to be shown to a wider audience.

Personalization: Algorithms use user data to personalize content feeds, showing users posts that align with their interests and past interactions. This ensures that users see content relevant to them, increasing engagement.

Frequency and Recency: The frequency and recency of posts also play a role. Consistently posting fresh content keeps the audience engaged and signals the algorithm to prioritize the brand's posts.

Adapting to Changes

To stay effective in the ever-changing algorithm landscape, marketers must adopt strategies to adapt and thrive:

Stay Updated: Regularly keep up with algorithm changes and platform updates. Following official platform blogs, industry news, and engaging with professional communities can provide insights into new developments.

Diversify Content Strategies: Diversify content formats and types to cater to different algorithm preferences. Combining videos, images, stories, and interactive posts ensures a well-rounded approach that can adapt to various algorithm changes.

Engagement Focus: Prioritize content that drives engagement. Encouraging likes, comments, shares, and saves can boost a post's visibility. Interactive content like polls, quizzes, and questions can also increase engagement.

Future Predictions

Predicting future algorithm changes involves understanding ongoing trends and technological advancements:

Increased Personalization: Algorithms will continue to become more sophisticated, offering highly personalized content experiences. Leveraging AI and machine learning, platforms will better understand user preferences and behaviors.

Real-Time Adjustments: Future algorithms may incorporate real-time adjustments based on user interactions. This means that content could dynamically change its visibility based on immediate user feedback.

Enhanced Transparency: There may be a push for greater transparency in how algorithms work. Users and marketers alike may demand clearer explanations of why certain content is prioritized, leading to more transparent and ethical algorithm practices.

Chapter 5

Ethical Considerations and
Social Responsibility

Branch 1: Addressing Misinformation

The Problem of Misinformation

Misinformation on social media platforms has become a critical issue, undermining public trust and creating widespread confusion:

Impact on Public Trust: Misinformation can erode trust in media, institutions, and even social relationships. False information spreads rapidly on social media due to its viral nature, leading to misinformed decisions and actions.

Examples of Harm: The spread of misinformation has had severe consequences, such as health-related myths during the COVID-19 pandemic, which affected public health responses and vaccination efforts.

Strategies for Combatting Misinformation

To effectively combat misinformation, several strategies can be employed:

Fact-Checking: Implementing robust fact-checking mechanisms can help identify and correct false information. Platforms like Facebook and Twitter have partnered with fact-checking organizations to label or remove false content.

Promoting Credible Sources: Encouraging the sharing and promotion of credible sources helps ensure that accurate information reaches the public. This can be achieved through algorithmic adjustments and partnerships with reputable news organizations.

Media Literacy Campaigns: Educating users about identifying misinformation is crucial. Media literacy campaigns can empower users to critically evaluate the information they encounter online.

Future Solutions

Looking ahead, innovative solutions can enhance efforts to address misinformation:

AI-Driven Detection: Artificial intelligence can play a significant role in detecting and flagging misinformation in real-time. Advanced algorithms can analyze patterns and identify potentially false content faster than human moderators.

Collaboration Between Platforms and Regulators:

Effective solutions will likely involve collaboration between social media platforms and regulatory bodies. Joint efforts can create standardized approaches to misinformation and enforce accountability.

Branch 2: Promoting Diversity and Inclusion

The Importance of Diversity

Diversity and inclusion in social media marketing are essential for creating a more equitable and representative digital environment:

Representation Matters: Diverse representation in marketing helps ensure that all audiences feel seen and valued. It fosters a sense of belonging and promotes positive social change.

Business Benefits: Brands that prioritize diversity and inclusion often see enhanced creativity, broader audience reach, and increased customer loyalty. Consumers are increasingly choosing to support brands that reflect their values.

Best Practices

To promote diversity and inclusion effectively, brands can adopt several best practices:

Authentic Representation: Ensure that marketing campaigns authentically represent diverse groups. This means avoiding stereotypes and ensuring that diverse voices are involved in the content creation process.

Inclusive Content Creation: Develop content that speaks to a wide range of experiences and perspectives. This includes using inclusive language, diverse visuals, and stories that resonate with various demographics.

Internal Practices: Promote diversity within the organization by hiring diverse talent and fostering an inclusive workplace culture. Internal diversity can lead to more authentic and resonant marketing efforts.

Looking Ahead

Future trends in diversity and inclusion will continue to evolve, with social media playing a key role:

Fostering Social Change: Social media will increasingly be used as a platform for social justice and advocacy. Brands that align with and support social causes will likely see stronger connections with their audiences.

Tech-Enabled Inclusion: Advances in technology, such as AI and machine learning, can help create more inclusive marketing by identifying and mitigating biases in content and advertising algorithms.

Branch 3: Balancing Profit and Purpose

Purpose-Driven Marketing

Purpose-driven marketing focuses on aligning business practices with broader social and environmental goals:

Importance in Modern Marketing: Consumers are increasingly valuing brands that prioritize purpose alongside profit. Purpose-driven marketing can enhance brand reputation, customer loyalty, and long-term success.

Key Elements: Successful purpose-driven marketing involves clear communication of the brand's values, consistent actions that align with these values, and genuine engagement with social and environmental issues.

Case Studies

Several brands have successfully balanced profit and purpose, serving as examples for others:

Patagonia: Known for its environmental activism, Patagonia integrates sustainability into every aspect of its business. The company's commitment to reducing its environmental footprint resonates with eco-conscious consumers and enhances brand loyalty.

Ben & Jerry's: This ice cream brand actively engages in social justice initiatives, from climate change to racial equality. Its purpose-driven campaigns have strengthened its connection with socially conscious consumers while driving sales.

TOMS Shoes: TOMS' "One for One" model, where the company donates a pair of shoes for every pair sold, exemplifies how purpose-driven initiatives can drive both social impact and business success.

Future Perspectives

The future of purpose-driven marketing will see deeper integration of sustainability and ethical considerations into core business strategies:

Sustainability as a Core Value: Sustainability will become a fundamental aspect of business operations, from supply chain practices to product development. Brands will need to demonstrate genuine commitment to environmental stewardship.

Ethical Considerations: Ethical business practices, including fair labor, transparent sourcing, and ethical treatment of employees and customers, will be crucial. Consumers will increasingly demand accountability and ethical behavior from brands.

Holistic Approach: A holistic approach to purpose-driven marketing will involve integrating social and environmental goals into the overall business strategy, ensuring that purpose and profit are mutually reinforcing.

The End!